Table of Contents

Introduction.. 1
Chapter 1: Gumbo..2
Chapter 2: Jambalaya..................................5
Chapter 3: Crawfish Étouffée.......................8
Chapter 4: Boudin...................................... 11
Chapter 5: Red Beans and Rice................14
Chapter 6: Shrimp Creole..........................17
Chapter 7: Cajun Fried Chicken................ 20
Chapter 8: Po' Boy Sandwich................... 23
Chapter 9: Dirty Rice................................. 26
Chapter 10: Crawfish Boil......................... 29
Chapter 11: Maque Choux........................32
Chapter 12: Cajun Boiled Peanuts........... 34
Chapter 13: Catfish Courtbouillon............. 36
Chapter 14: Tasso Ham............................ 39
Chapter 15: Cajun Shrimp and Grits........ 42
Chapter 16: Cajun Meatloaf......................45
Chapter 17: Chicken and Sausage Sauce Piquante...48
Chapter 18: Andouille Sausage................ 51
Chapter 19: Beignets................................ 54
Chapter 20: Crawfish Pie..........................57
Conclusion.. 60

Introduction

Welcome to "20 Classic Cajun Dishes," where we celebrate the bold, flavorful, and soulful cuisine of Louisiana. Cajun cooking is a testament to the resourcefulness and creativity of the Cajun people, who have perfected the art of turning simple, humble ingredients into dishes bursting with flavor. This cookbook is a tribute to that heritage, offering you a selection of twenty quintessential Cajun recipes that have stood the test of time.

In these pages, you will find everything from the rich and hearty gumbo to the spicy and satisfying jambalaya, as well as lesser-known but equally delicious dishes like Maque Choux and Tasso Ham. Each recipe is crafted to bring out the authentic taste of Cajun cuisine, with step-by-step instructions that make the cooking process enjoyable and accessible.

Whether you're cooking for a special occasion or simply want to bring a taste of Louisiana into your home, "20 Classic Cajun Dishes" is your guide to mastering these iconic recipes. So, grab your apron, gather your ingredients, and let's dive into the world of Cajun cooking!

Chapter 1: Gumbo

A rich, hearty stew made with a roux base, often featuring chicken, sausage, and seafood, served over rice.

Ingredients:

- 1/2 cup vegetable oil
- 1/2 cup all-purpose flour
- 1 large onion, finely chopped
- 1 bell pepper, finely chopped
- 2 celery stalks, finely chopped
- 4 cloves garlic, minced
- 1 pound smoked sausage, sliced
- 1 pound chicken thighs, boneless and skinless, cut into bite-sized pieces
- 1 pound raw shrimp, peeled and deveined
- 1 quart chicken broth
- 2 cups water
- 1 (14.5 oz) can diced tomatoes
- 2 bay leaves
- 1 tablespoon Cajun seasoning
- 1 teaspoon dried thyme
- 1/2 teaspoon cayenne pepper (optional)
- 2 cups sliced okra (fresh or frozen)
- Salt and pepper to taste
- 4 cups cooked white rice
- Chopped green onions and parsley for garnish

Cooking Instructions:

1. Make the Roux:
    - In a large, heavy-bottomed pot or Dutch oven, heat the vegetable oil over medium heat. Gradually whisk in the flour until smooth.
    - Cook the roux, whisking constantly, until it turns a deep brown color (the color of chocolate), about 20-30 minutes. Be careful not to let it burn.
2. Add the Vegetables:
    - Add the chopped onion, bell pepper, and celery to the roux. Cook, stirring frequently, until the vegetables are soft, about 5-7 minutes.
    - Stir in the minced garlic and cook for another minute.
3. Cook the Meats:
    - Add the sliced sausage and chicken pieces to the pot. Cook until the chicken is browned on all sides, about 5 minutes.
4. Simmer the Gumbo:
    - Pour in the chicken broth, water, and diced tomatoes. Add the bay leaves, Cajun seasoning, dried thyme, and cayenne pepper (if using).
    - Bring the mixture to a boil, then reduce the heat to low and let it simmer for about 45 minutes, stirring occasionally.
5. Add the Shrimp and Okra:
    - Stir in the shrimp and sliced okra. Simmer for another 15 minutes, or

    until the shrimp is cooked through and the okra is tender.
    - Season with salt and pepper to taste.
6. Serve:
    - Remove the bay leaves and discard them.
    - Serve the gumbo over cooked white rice.
    - Garnish with chopped green onions and parsley.

Chapter 2: Jambalaya

A flavorful rice dish cooked with a variety of meats like chicken, sausage, and shrimp, seasoned with Cajun spices.

Ingredients:

- 2 tablespoons vegetable oil
- 1 pound chicken thighs, boneless and skinless, cut into bite-sized pieces
- 1 pound smoked sausage, sliced
- 1 large onion, finely chopped
- 1 bell pepper, finely chopped
- 2 celery stalks, finely chopped
- 4 cloves garlic, minced
- 1 (14.5 oz) can diced tomatoes
- 1 tablespoon tomato paste
- 2 cups long-grain rice
- 4 cups chicken broth
- 1 tablespoon Cajun seasoning
- 1 teaspoon dried thyme
- 1/2 teaspoon smoked paprika
- 1/2 teaspoon cayenne pepper (optional)
- 1 pound raw shrimp, peeled and deveined
- 1/2 cup chopped green onions
- Salt and pepper to taste
- Chopped parsley for garnish

Cooking Instructions:

1. Cook the Chicken and Sausage:
    - In a large pot or Dutch oven, heat the vegetable oil over medium-high heat. Add the chicken pieces and

sausage slices, cooking until the chicken is browned on all sides and the sausage is lightly browned, about 5-7 minutes.
    - Remove the chicken and sausage from the pot and set them aside.
2. Sauté the Vegetables:
    - In the same pot, add the chopped onion, bell pepper, and celery. Cook, stirring frequently, until the vegetables are softened, about 5 minutes.
    - Add the minced garlic and cook for another minute.
3. Add the Tomatoes and Rice:
    - Stir in the diced tomatoes (with their juices) and tomato paste, mixing well.
    - Add the rice and cook, stirring constantly, for about 2 minutes to lightly toast the rice.
4. Simmer the Jambalaya:
    - Pour in the chicken broth, and add the Cajun seasoning, dried thyme, smoked paprika, and cayenne pepper (if using). Stir well to combine.
    - Return the cooked chicken and sausage to the pot. Bring the mixture to a boil, then reduce the heat to low, cover, and simmer for about 20-25 minutes, or until the rice is tender and has absorbed most of the liquid.
5. Add the Shrimp:
    - Gently stir in the shrimp and green onions. Cover and cook for another

- 5-7 minutes, or until the shrimp are pink and cooked through.
- ○ Season with salt and pepper to taste.
6. Serve:
    - ○ Remove the pot from heat and let it sit, covered, for about 5 minutes.
    - ○ Fluff the jambalaya with a fork, then serve.
    - ○ Garnish with chopped parsley.

Chapter 3: Crawfish Étouffée

A savory stew made with crawfish smothered in a roux-based sauce, served over rice.

Ingredients:

- 2 pounds crawfish tails (peeled, with fat reserved if available)
- 1/2 cup butter
- 1/2 cup all-purpose flour
- 1 large onion, finely chopped
- 1 bell pepper, finely chopped
- 3 celery stalks, finely chopped
- 4 cloves garlic, minced
- 2 cups chicken or seafood stock
- 1 cup tomato sauce
- 1 tablespoon Worcestershire sauce
- 1 teaspoon hot sauce (like Tabasco)
- 2 bay leaves
- 1 teaspoon paprika
- 1/2 teaspoon cayenne pepper (adjust to taste)
- Salt and black pepper to taste
- 2 green onions, chopped
- 2 tablespoons fresh parsley, chopped
- Cooked white rice, for serving

Cooking Instructions:

1. Prepare the Roux:
    - In a large skillet or heavy-bottomed pot, melt the butter over medium heat.

- Once melted, add the flour gradually, stirring constantly to avoid lumps.
- Cook the roux, stirring continuously, until it turns a light brown color, about 10-15 minutes.

2. Cook the Vegetables:
    - Add the chopped onion, bell pepper, celery, and garlic to the roux.
    - Sauté the vegetables until they are soft and the onion is translucent, about 8-10 minutes.
3. Add the Liquids:
    - Gradually pour in the chicken or seafood stock, stirring constantly to combine with the roux and vegetables.
    - Add the tomato sauce, Worcestershire sauce, and hot sauce. Stir well to combine.
4. Season and Simmer:
    - Add the bay leaves, paprika, cayenne pepper, salt, and black pepper.
    - Reduce the heat to low and let the mixture simmer for about 20 minutes, stirring occasionally to prevent sticking.
5. Add the Crawfish:
    - Add the crawfish tails and any reserved crawfish fat to the pot. Stir to combine.
    - Let the crawfish cook in the sauce for another 10-15 minutes, until they are heated through and the flavors meld together.

6. Finish the Dish:
    - Stir in the chopped green onions and parsley.
    - Adjust seasoning with additional salt, pepper, or hot sauce if needed.
7. Serve:
    - Serve the Crawfish Étouffée over a bed of cooked white rice.

Chapter 4: Boudin

A type of Cajun sausage stuffed with a mixture of pork, rice, and spices.

Ingredients:

- 2 pounds pork shoulder, cut into chunks
- 1 pound pork liver, cut into chunks
- 1 large onion, chopped
- 1 bell pepper, chopped
- 3 celery stalks, chopped
- 4 cloves garlic, minced
- 1 cup long-grain white rice
- 4 cups water or chicken stock
- 1 teaspoon salt
- 1 teaspoon black pepper
- 1 teaspoon cayenne pepper
- 1 teaspoon paprika
- 1 teaspoon dried thyme
- 1 teaspoon dried oregano
- 1/2 cup chopped green onions
- 1/2 cup chopped fresh parsley
- Sausage casings (if stuffing)
- Optional: Crusty bread or crackers for serving

Cooking Instructions:

1. Cook the Meat and Vegetables:
    - In a large pot, combine the pork shoulder, pork liver, onion, bell pepper, celery, and garlic.
    - Add enough water or chicken stock to cover the ingredients.

- Bring to a boil, then reduce the heat and simmer until the meat is tender, about 1.5 to 2 hours.
2. Cook the Rice:
    - While the meat is cooking, cook the rice in a separate pot according to the package instructions.
    - Set aside.
3. Grind the Meat and Vegetables:
    - Once the meat is tender, remove it from the pot and let it cool slightly.
    - Reserve the cooking liquid.
    - Using a meat grinder or food processor, grind the cooked meat and vegetables together until finely ground.
4. Combine Ingredients:
    - In a large mixing bowl, combine the ground meat and vegetables with the cooked rice.
    - Add 1 cup of the reserved cooking liquid to the mixture.
    - Season with salt, black pepper, cayenne pepper, paprika, thyme, and oregano.
    - Stir in the chopped green onions and parsley. Mix well until all ingredients are thoroughly combined.
5. Stuff the Sausage Casings:
    - If using sausage casings, rinse them thoroughly in cold water.
    - Using a sausage stuffer, fill the casings with the boudin mixture.
    - Be careful not to overfill the casings to prevent them from bursting.

6. Cook the Boudin:
    - To cook the boudin, you can either steam or poach the sausages until they are heated through, about 15-20 minutes.
    - Alternatively, you can grill or pan-fry the boudin until the casing is browned and crispy.
7. Serve:
    - Serve the boudin hot, either on its own or with crusty bread or crackers.

Chapter 5: Red Beans and Rice

Slow-cooked red beans with ham hocks or sausage, served over a bed of white rice.

Ingredients:

For the Red Beans:

- 1 pound dried red kidney beans
- 2 tablespoons vegetable oil
- 1 large onion, finely chopped
- 1 green bell pepper, finely chopped
- 1 celery stalk, finely chopped
- 4 garlic cloves, minced
- 1 pound smoked sausage, sliced into rounds
- 1 ham hock (optional, for added flavor)
- 2 teaspoons dried thyme
- 1 teaspoon dried oregano
- 1 teaspoon paprika
- 1 teaspoon cayenne pepper (adjust to taste)
- 2 bay leaves
- 6 cups water or chicken broth
- Salt and black pepper to taste

For the Rice:

- 2 cups long-grain white rice
- 4 cups water
- 1 tablespoon butter or vegetable oil
- 1/2 teaspoon salt

Cooking Instructions:

1. **Prepare the Beans:**
    - Sort through the dried beans to remove any debris, then rinse them thoroughly under cold water.
    - Place the beans in a large bowl and cover with water. Allow them to soak overnight. Alternatively, for a quicker method, bring the beans and water to a boil for 2 minutes, then remove from heat, cover, and let sit for 1 hour. Drain and rinse the beans.
2. **Cook the Red Beans:**
    - In a large pot or Dutch oven, heat the vegetable oil over medium-high heat.
    - Add the chopped onion, bell pepper, and celery. Sauté until the vegetables are tender and the onion is translucent, about 5-7 minutes.
    - Stir in the minced garlic and cook for an additional 1 minute until fragrant.
    - Add the smoked sausage slices and ham hock (if using). Cook until the sausage is browned, about 5 minutes.
    - Stir in the soaked beans, thyme, oregano, paprika, cayenne pepper, and bay leaves.
    - Pour in the water or chicken broth, stirring to combine. Bring to a boil.
    - Once boiling, reduce the heat to low, cover, and simmer for 2 to 2.5 hours, or until the beans are tender and creamy. Stir occasionally, and if the

mixture becomes too thick, add more water or broth as needed.
- Remove the ham hock and bay leaves. Season with salt and black pepper to taste.

3. **Prepare the Rice:**
   - While the beans are cooking, prepare the rice. In a medium saucepan, bring 4 cups of water to a boil.
   - Add the rice, butter or vegetable oil, and salt. Stir well.
   - Reduce the heat to low, cover, and simmer for 18-20 minutes, or until the rice is tender and the water is absorbed.
   - Remove from heat and let sit, covered, for an additional 5 minutes. Fluff with a fork before serving.

4. **Serve:**
   - Spoon a generous serving of the red beans over a bed of fluffy white rice.
   - Garnish with chopped green onions or parsley if desired.
   - Serve hot, accompanied by cornbread or French bread.

Chapter 6: Shrimp Creole

A tomato-based dish with shrimp, peppers, onions, and celery, seasoned with Creole spices, served over rice.

Ingredients:

- 2 pounds large shrimp, peeled and deveined
- 2 tablespoons vegetable oil
- 1 large onion, finely chopped
- 1 green bell pepper, finely chopped
- 2 celery stalks, finely chopped
- 4 garlic cloves, minced
- 1 (14.5-ounce) can diced tomatoes
- 1 (8-ounce) can tomato sauce
- 2 tablespoons tomato paste
- 1 cup chicken broth
- 1 teaspoon dried thyme
- 1 teaspoon dried oregano
- 1 teaspoon paprika
- 1/2 teaspoon cayenne pepper (adjust to taste)
- 2 bay leaves
- 1 teaspoon Worcestershire sauce
- Salt and black pepper to taste
- 1/2 cup chopped green onions (for garnish)
- 2 tablespoons chopped fresh parsley (for garnish)
- Cooked white rice (for serving)

Cooking Instructions:

1. **Prepare the Shrimp:**
   - Rinse the peeled and deveined shrimp under cold water and pat dry with paper towels. Set aside.
2. **Cook the Vegetables:**
   - In a large skillet or Dutch oven, heat the vegetable oil over medium-high heat.
   - Add the chopped onion, bell pepper, and celery. Sauté until the vegetables are tender and the onion is translucent, about 5-7 minutes.
   - Stir in the minced garlic and cook for an additional 1 minute until fragrant.
3. **Prepare the Creole Sauce:**
   - Add the diced tomatoes (with their juice), tomato sauce, and tomato paste to the skillet. Stir to combine.
   - Pour in the chicken broth and stir well.
   - Add the thyme, oregano, paprika, cayenne pepper, and bay leaves. Stir to incorporate the spices into the sauce.
   - Bring the mixture to a boil, then reduce the heat to low and let it simmer for 20-30 minutes, allowing the flavors to meld and the sauce to thicken slightly. Stir occasionally to prevent sticking.
4. **Cook the Shrimp:**
   - After the sauce has simmered, add the shrimp to the skillet. Cook for 5-7

minutes, or until the shrimp are pink and opaque, stirring occasionally.
- Stir in the Worcestershire sauce and season with salt and black pepper to taste. Remove and discard the bay leaves.

5. **Serve:**
   - Serve the Shrimp Creole hot over a bed of cooked white rice.
   - Garnish with chopped green onions and fresh parsley.
   - Enjoy with a side of French bread or a green salad.

Chapter 7: Cajun Fried Chicken

Crispy, spiced fried chicken marinated in buttermilk and Cajun seasoning.

Ingredients

- 4 boneless, skinless chicken breasts
- 2 cups buttermilk
- 1 tablespoon hot sauce
- 2 cups all-purpose flour
- 1 cup cornmeal
- 2 tablespoons Cajun seasoning (store-bought or homemade)
- 1 teaspoon garlic powder
- 1 teaspoon onion powder
- 1 teaspoon paprika
- 1/2 teaspoon cayenne pepper (optional for extra heat)
- 1 teaspoon salt
- 1/2 teaspoon black pepper
- 1 teaspoon baking powder
- Vegetable oil for frying

Instructions

1. **Marinate the Chicken:**
   - In a large bowl, mix the buttermilk and hot sauce. Add the chicken breasts, ensuring they are fully submerged. Cover the bowl with plastic wrap and refrigerate for at least 2 hours, or overnight for best results.

2. **Prepare the Breading:**
   - In a large shallow dish, combine the flour, cornmeal, Cajun seasoning, garlic powder, onion powder, paprika, cayenne pepper (if using), salt, black pepper, and baking powder. Mix well to ensure the spices are evenly distributed.
3. **Heat the Oil:**
   - Pour vegetable oil into a large, deep skillet or Dutch oven to a depth of about 2 inches. Heat the oil over medium-high heat until it reaches 350°F (175°C). Use a kitchen thermometer to monitor the temperature.
4. **Bread the Chicken:**
   - Remove the chicken from the buttermilk, allowing any excess to drip off. Dredge each piece in the flour mixture, pressing firmly to adhere the coating. Place the breaded chicken on a wire rack and let it rest for 10 minutes. This helps the coating stick better during frying.
5. **Fry the Chicken:**
   - Carefully place the chicken pieces into the hot oil, being careful not to overcrowd the pan. Fry in batches if necessary. Cook for about 6-8 minutes per side, or until the chicken is golden brown and cooked through (internal temperature should reach 165°F or 74°C). Adjust the heat as

needed to maintain the oil temperature.
6. **Drain and Serve:**
    - Use a slotted spoon or tongs to transfer the fried chicken to a paper towel-lined plate to drain any excess oil. Let the chicken rest for a few minutes before serving to ensure it stays crispy.
7. **Serve:**
    - Serve your Cajun fried chicken hot, with sides like coleslaw, potato salad, or cornbread. Enjoy the delicious, spicy, and crispy chicken!

Chapter 8: Po' Boy Sandwich

A traditional Louisiana sandwich typically filled with fried seafood or roast beef, served on a baguette.

Ingredients

- 1 pound shrimp, peeled and deveined (or use oysters, catfish, or roast beef)
- 2 cups buttermilk
- 2 cups all-purpose flour
- 1 cup cornmeal
- 2 tablespoons Cajun seasoning (store-bought or homemade)
- 1 teaspoon garlic powder
- 1 teaspoon onion powder
- 1 teaspoon paprika
- 1/2 teaspoon cayenne pepper (optional for extra heat)
- 1 teaspoon salt
- 1/2 teaspoon black pepper
- 4 French bread rolls or baguettes, sliced lengthwise
- Shredded lettuce
- Sliced tomatoes
- Dill pickles, sliced
- 1/2 cup mayonnaise
- 2 tablespoons Creole mustard
- Hot sauce, to taste
- Vegetable oil for frying

Instructions

1. **Marinate the Shrimp:**
   - In a large bowl, mix the buttermilk and hot sauce. Add the shrimp (or other protein), ensuring they are fully submerged. Cover the bowl with plastic wrap and refrigerate for at least 30 minutes.
2. **Prepare the Breading:**
   - In a large shallow dish, combine the flour, cornmeal, Cajun seasoning, garlic powder, onion powder, paprika, cayenne pepper (if using), salt, and black pepper. Mix well to ensure the spices are evenly distributed.
3. **Heat the Oil:**
   - Pour vegetable oil into a large, deep skillet or Dutch oven to a depth of about 2 inches. Heat the oil over medium-high heat until it reaches 350°F (175°C). Use a kitchen thermometer to monitor the temperature.
4. **Bread the Shrimp:**
   - Remove the shrimp from the buttermilk, allowing any excess to drip off. Dredge each piece in the flour mixture, pressing firmly to adhere the coating. Place the breaded shrimp on a wire rack and let it rest for 10 minutes. This helps the coating stick better during frying.

5. **Fry the Shrimp:**
    - Carefully place the shrimp into the hot oil, being careful not to overcrowd the pan. Fry in batches if necessary. Cook for about 2-3 minutes per side, or until the shrimp are golden brown and cooked through. Adjust the heat as needed to maintain the oil temperature.
6. **Drain and Prepare the Sandwich:**
    - Use a slotted spoon or tongs to transfer the fried shrimp to a paper towel-lined plate to drain any excess oil. Let the shrimp rest for a few minutes before assembling the sandwich.
7. **Assemble the Po' Boy:**
    - In a small bowl, mix the mayonnaise and Creole mustard. Spread this mixture on both sides of the French bread rolls or baguettes. Add a layer of shredded lettuce, followed by slices of tomatoes and dill pickles. Top with the fried shrimp. Drizzle with additional hot sauce if desired.
8. **Serve:**
    - Serve the Po' Boy sandwiches immediately while the shrimp are still hot and crispy. Enjoy with a side of chips, fries, or a cold beverage.

Chapter 9: Dirty Rice

A spicy rice dish cooked with ground meat, chicken livers, and a blend of Cajun seasonings.

Ingredients:

- 1 lb chicken livers, finely chopped
- 1 lb ground pork
- 1/2 lb chicken gizzards, finely chopped
- 1 cup finely chopped onions
- 1/2 cup finely chopped bell peppers
- 1/2 cup finely chopped celery
- 4 cloves garlic, minced
- 2 cups long-grain white rice
- 4 cups chicken broth
- 2 tbsp vegetable oil
- 1 tbsp Cajun seasoning
- 1 tsp dried thyme
- 1 tsp dried oregano
- 1 tsp paprika
- 1/2 tsp cayenne pepper (optional, for extra heat)
- 2 green onions, chopped (for garnish)
- Salt and black pepper to taste

Instructions:

1. **Cook the Rice:**
    - Rinse the rice under cold water until the water runs clear. This helps remove excess starch and keeps the rice from being too sticky.
    - In a medium pot, bring the chicken broth to a boil. Add the rice, reduce

the heat to low, cover, and simmer for about 18-20 minutes or until the rice is tender and has absorbed all the liquid. Remove from heat and let it sit, covered, for another 5 minutes. Fluff with a fork and set aside.
2. **Prepare the Meat:**
    - In a large skillet or Dutch oven, heat the vegetable oil over medium-high heat. Add the ground pork, chicken livers, and gizzards. Cook, breaking up the meat with a spoon, until browned and cooked through, about 8-10 minutes.
3. **Add Vegetables:**
    - Add the chopped onions, bell peppers, and celery to the meat mixture. Cook, stirring occasionally, until the vegetables are soft, about 5-7 minutes.
    - Add the minced garlic and cook for an additional 2 minutes, until fragrant.
4. **Season the Mixture:**
    - Stir in the Cajun seasoning, thyme, oregano, paprika, cayenne pepper (if using), salt, and black pepper. Cook for another 2-3 minutes to allow the spices to blend.
5. **Combine with Rice:**
    - Add the cooked rice to the meat and vegetable mixture. Stir well to combine, ensuring the rice is evenly coated with the seasonings and mixed with the meat and vegetables.

6. **Serve:**
    - Remove from heat and let the dirty rice rest for a few minutes. Garnish with chopped green onions before serving.

Chapter 10: Crawfish Boil

Fresh crawfish boiled with potatoes, corn, and Cajun spices, often enjoyed with friends and family.

Ingredients:

- 10 lbs live crawfish
- 2 lbs small red potatoes, halved
- 1 lb smoked sausage, sliced into 1-inch pieces
- 6 ears of corn, shucked and cut into thirds
- 4 lemons, halved
- 4 large onions, quartered
- 2 heads of garlic, halved horizontally
- 4 bay leaves
- 1/4 cup Zatarain's Crawfish, Shrimp & Crab Boil seasoning (or similar)
- 1/4 cup salt
- 1/4 cup black peppercorns
- 1/4 cup cayenne pepper
- 1/4 cup paprika
- 1/4 cup dried thyme
- 1/4 cup dried oregano
- 1/4 cup crushed red pepper flakes
- 1 stick unsalted butter
- 3 gallons water

Instructions:

1. **Prepare the Crawfish:**
     - Rinse the live crawfish thoroughly under cold water to remove any dirt and debris. Place them in a large cooler or tub filled with clean, cold

water to purge any impurities. Let them sit for about 20-30 minutes, then rinse again.
2. **Boil the Water:**
    - In a large pot or boiling pot (at least 20-30 quarts), bring 3 gallons of water to a rolling boil. Add the Zatarain's seasoning, salt, black peppercorns, cayenne pepper, paprika, thyme, oregano, and crushed red pepper flakes. Squeeze the juice from the lemon halves into the pot, then toss in the lemon halves themselves. Add the bay leaves and bring the mixture back to a boil.
3. **Cook the Vegetables:**
    - Add the potatoes, onions, garlic, and sausage to the boiling water. Cook for about 10-15 minutes, or until the potatoes are just tender.
4. **Add the Corn:**
    - Add the corn pieces and cook for an additional 5 minutes.
5. **Cook the Crawfish:**
    - Carefully add the live crawfish to the pot. Stir gently to ensure they are fully submerged. Cook for about 3-5 minutes, or until the crawfish turn bright red and float to the top.
6. **Soak the Crawfish:**
    - Turn off the heat and let the crawfish soak in the seasoned water for 15-20 minutes. This allows them to absorb the flavors. If you prefer

spicier crawfish, let them soak longer.
7. **Drain and Serve:**
    o Carefully drain the water from the pot. Transfer the crawfish, potatoes, corn, sausage, onions, and garlic to a large serving platter or spread out on a newspaper-covered table for a traditional presentation.
8. **Add Butter:**
    o Melt the unsalted butter and drizzle it over the crawfish and vegetables for added flavor.
9. **Enjoy:**
    o Serve the crawfish boil hot, with additional lemon wedges and dipping sauces as desired. Enjoy the feast with friends and family!

Chapter 11: Maque Choux

A sautéed corn dish with bell peppers, onions, and tomatoes, often served as a side.

Ingredients:

- 6 ears of corn, shucked and kernels removed
- 2 tablespoons unsalted butter
- 2 tablespoons vegetable oil
- 1 large onion, finely chopped
- 1 green bell pepper, finely chopped
- 1 red bell pepper, finely chopped
- 2 celery stalks, finely chopped
- 3 cloves garlic, minced
- 1 cup diced tomatoes (canned or fresh)
- 1 cup heavy cream
- 1 teaspoon Cajun seasoning
- 1/2 teaspoon smoked paprika
- 1/4 teaspoon cayenne pepper (optional)
- Salt and pepper to taste
- 1/4 cup chopped green onions
- 1/4 cup chopped fresh parsley

Cooking Instructions:

1. **Prepare the Corn:**
   - Shuck the corn and remove the kernels using a sharp knife. Set the kernels aside.
2. **Sauté the Vegetables:**
   - In a large skillet or Dutch oven, heat the butter and vegetable oil over medium heat.

- Add the chopped onion, green bell pepper, red bell pepper, and celery. Cook, stirring frequently, until the vegetables are soft, about 5-7 minutes.
- Add the minced garlic and cook for another minute.
3. **Cook the Corn:**
   - Add the corn kernels to the skillet, stirring to combine with the sautéed vegetables.
   - Cook for about 5 minutes, allowing the corn to slightly caramelize.
4. **Add Tomatoes and Seasonings:**
   - Stir in the diced tomatoes and cook for another 2-3 minutes.
   - Add the Cajun seasoning, smoked paprika, and cayenne pepper (if using). Stir well to combine.
5. **Simmer with Cream:**
   - Pour in the heavy cream and bring the mixture to a simmer.
   - Reduce the heat to low and cook for about 10-15 minutes, stirring occasionally, until the mixture thickens and the flavors meld together.
6. **Finish and Serve:**
   - Season with salt and pepper to taste.
   - Stir in the chopped green onions and parsley just before serving.
   - Serve warm as a side dish.

Chapter 12: Cajun Boiled Peanuts

Green peanuts boiled in a briny, spicy mixture until tender.

Ingredients:

- 2 pounds raw green peanuts (in the shell)
- 1/2 cup kosher salt
- 1/4 cup Cajun seasoning
- 2 tablespoons garlic powder
- 2 tablespoons onion powder
- 1 tablespoon smoked paprika
- 1 tablespoon cayenne pepper (optional)
- 3-4 bay leaves
- 10 cups water (or enough to cover the peanuts)

Cooking Instructions:

1. **Rinse the Peanuts:**
   - Thoroughly rinse the raw green peanuts under cold water to remove any dirt and debris.
2. **Prepare the Boiling Liquid:**
   - In a large pot, add the water, kosher salt, Cajun seasoning, garlic powder, onion powder, smoked paprika, cayenne pepper (if using), and bay leaves.
   - Stir to combine and bring the mixture to a boil over high heat.

3. **Add the Peanuts:**
    - Add the rinsed peanuts to the boiling liquid. Ensure they are fully submerged.
4. **Boil the Peanuts:**
    - Reduce the heat to medium-low and cover the pot.
    - Simmer the peanuts for 2-3 hours, or until they reach your desired level of tenderness. Stir occasionally and add more water if necessary to keep the peanuts submerged.
5. **Taste and Adjust Seasoning:**
    - After about 2 hours, taste a peanut to check for doneness and seasoning. If needed, add more salt or Cajun seasoning to the boiling liquid.
    - Continue to simmer until the peanuts are soft and flavorful.
6. **Cool and Serve:**
    - Once the peanuts are fully cooked, remove the pot from heat and let them cool in the brine for at least 30 minutes to absorb more flavor.
    - Serve the boiled peanuts warm or at room temperature, draining off excess brine before eating.

Chapter 13: Catfish Courtbouillon

A tomato-based fish stew with catfish, onions, peppers, and a blend of Cajun spices.

Ingredients:

- 4-6 catfish fillets (about 2 pounds)
- 1/2 cup vegetable oil
- 1/2 cup all-purpose flour
- 1 large onion, finely chopped
- 1 bell pepper, finely chopped
- 3 celery stalks, finely chopped
- 4 cloves garlic, minced
- 1 (14.5-ounce) can diced tomatoes
- 1 (6-ounce) can tomato paste
- 4 cups seafood or chicken stock
- 1/2 cup dry white wine
- 2 bay leaves
- 1 teaspoon dried thyme
- 1 teaspoon dried oregano
- 1 teaspoon paprika
- 1/2 teaspoon cayenne pepper (adjust to taste)
- Salt and black pepper to taste
- 2 green onions, chopped
- 2 tablespoons fresh parsley, chopped
- Cooked white rice, for serving
- Lemon wedges, for garnish

Cooking Instructions:

1. **Prepare the Roux:**
   - In a large, heavy-bottomed pot or Dutch oven, heat the vegetable oil over medium heat.
   - Gradually add the flour, stirring constantly to prevent lumps.
   - Cook the roux, stirring continuously, until it reaches a medium brown color, about 10-15 minutes.
2. **Cook the Vegetables:**
   - Add the chopped onion, bell pepper, and celery to the roux.
   - Sauté the vegetables until they are soft and the onion is translucent, about 8-10 minutes.
   - Add the minced garlic and cook for an additional 1-2 minutes.
3. **Add the Liquids and Seasonings:**
   - Stir in the diced tomatoes (with juice), tomato paste, seafood or chicken stock, and white wine.
   - Add the bay leaves, thyme, oregano, paprika, cayenne pepper, salt, and black pepper.
   - Bring the mixture to a boil, then reduce the heat and let it simmer for 30 minutes, stirring occasionally.
4. **Cook the Catfish:**
   - Add the catfish fillets to the pot, making sure they are submerged in the sauce.
   - Simmer the courtbouillon until the fish is cooked through and flakes

easily with a fork, about 15-20 minutes.
5. **Finish the Dish:**
    - Stir in the chopped green onions and parsley.
    - Adjust seasoning with additional salt, pepper, or cayenne if needed.
6. **Serve:**
    - Serve the Catfish Courtbouillon over a bed of cooked white rice.
    - Garnish with lemon wedges.

Chapter 14: Tasso Ham

Spicy, cured pork shoulder, often used to flavor dishes like gumbo and jambalaya.

Ingredients:

- 2 pounds pork shoulder or butt, cut into 1/2-inch thick slices
- 2 tablespoons paprika
- 1 tablespoon salt
- 1 tablespoon black pepper
- 1 tablespoon white pepper
- 1 tablespoon cayenne pepper
- 1 tablespoon dried oregano
- 1 tablespoon dried thyme
- 1 teaspoon garlic powder
- 1 teaspoon onion powder
- 1 teaspoon ground mustard
- 1 teaspoon crushed red pepper flakes
- 1 tablespoon brown sugar

Cooking Instructions:

1. **Prepare the Spice Rub:**
    - In a small bowl, combine the paprika, salt, black pepper, white pepper, cayenne pepper, oregano, thyme, garlic powder, onion powder, ground mustard, crushed red pepper flakes, and brown sugar.
    - Mix well to create the spice rub.

2. **Season the Pork:**
    - Rub the spice mixture generously all over the pork slices, making sure they are evenly coated.
    - Place the seasoned pork slices on a baking sheet or in a shallow dish.
    - Cover and refrigerate for at least 4 hours, preferably overnight, to allow the flavors to penetrate the meat.
3. **Smoke the Pork:**
    - Preheat your smoker to 225°F (107°C). If you don't have a smoker, you can use a grill with indirect heat or an oven with a low temperature setting.
    - Place the pork slices in the smoker and smoke for 3-4 hours, or until the meat reaches an internal temperature of 150°F (65°C).
    - If using a grill or oven, cook the pork on a wire rack set over a baking sheet to allow for proper air circulation.
4. **Cool and Store:**
    - Remove the Tasso Ham from the smoker and let it cool to room temperature.
    - Wrap the cooled Tasso Ham tightly in plastic wrap or aluminum foil.
    - Store in the refrigerator for up to 1 week or in the freezer for up to 3 months.
5. **Serve:**
    - Tasso Ham can be used to flavor a variety of dishes, such as gumbo, jambalaya, red beans and rice, or

any recipe that calls for smoked pork.

Chapter 15: Cajun Shrimp and Grits

Creamy grits topped with sautéed shrimp in a spicy, savory sauce.

Ingredients:

For the Grits:

- 4 cups water
- 1 cup stone-ground grits
- 1 cup milk
- 1 cup shredded sharp cheddar cheese
- 2 tablespoons butter
- Salt and black pepper to taste

For the Cajun Shrimp:

- 1 pound large shrimp, peeled and deveined
- 2 tablespoons olive oil
- 1 tablespoon Cajun seasoning
- 1 teaspoon smoked paprika
- 1/2 teaspoon cayenne pepper (adjust to taste)
- 1/2 teaspoon garlic powder
- 1/2 teaspoon onion powder
- 1/4 teaspoon dried thyme
- 1/4 teaspoon dried oregano
- 1/4 teaspoon dried basil
- 1/4 teaspoon black pepper
- 2 tablespoons butter
- 2 garlic cloves, minced
- 1/4 cup chicken broth
- 1/4 cup heavy cream

- 2 tablespoons chopped fresh parsley (for garnish)
- 2 tablespoons chopped green onions (for garnish)

Cooking Instructions:

1. **Prepare the Grits:**
   - In a large pot, bring 4 cups of water to a boil.
   - Slowly whisk in the stone-ground grits to avoid lumps. Reduce the heat to low and cook, stirring occasionally, for about 20-25 minutes, or until the grits are thick and creamy.
   - Stir in the milk, shredded cheddar cheese, and butter. Continue to cook for an additional 5 minutes, stirring frequently until the cheese and butter are fully melted and incorporated.
   - Season with salt and black pepper to taste. Remove from heat and keep warm.
2. **Season the Shrimp:**
   - In a large bowl, toss the peeled and deveined shrimp with olive oil, Cajun seasoning, smoked paprika, cayenne pepper, garlic powder, onion powder, dried thyme, dried oregano, dried basil, and black pepper. Ensure the shrimp are evenly coated with the seasoning mixture.

3. **Cook the Shrimp:**
    - In a large skillet over medium-high heat, melt the butter.
    - Add the minced garlic and sauté for about 1 minute until fragrant.
    - Add the seasoned shrimp to the skillet in a single layer. Cook for 2-3 minutes on each side until the shrimp are pink and opaque. Remove the shrimp from the skillet and set aside.
4. **Make the Sauce:**
    - In the same skillet, add the chicken broth and heavy cream. Bring the mixture to a simmer, stirring frequently, until the sauce is slightly thickened, about 3-5 minutes.
5. **Combine and Serve:**
    - Return the cooked shrimp to the skillet, tossing to coat them in the sauce.
    - Serve the Cajun shrimp over a generous portion of creamy grits.
    - Garnish with chopped fresh parsley and green onions.
    - Serve immediately and enjoy!

Chapter 16: Cajun Meatloaf

A classic meatloaf spiced with Cajun seasoning, often including the holy trinity of bell peppers, onions, and celery.

Ingredients:

For the Meatloaf:

- 1 pound ground beef
- 1/2 pound ground pork
- 1/2 cup finely chopped onion
- 1/2 cup finely chopped green bell pepper
- 1/2 cup finely chopped celery
- 3 garlic cloves, minced
- 1/2 cup breadcrumbs
- 1/4 cup milk
- 2 large eggs, beaten
- 2 tablespoons Worcestershire sauce
- 1 tablespoon Cajun seasoning
- 1 teaspoon dried thyme
- 1 teaspoon dried oregano
- 1 teaspoon paprika
- 1/2 teaspoon cayenne pepper (adjust to taste)
- 1/2 teaspoon black pepper
- 1/2 teaspoon salt

For the Glaze:

- 1/2 cup ketchup
- 2 tablespoons brown sugar
- 1 tablespoon Dijon mustard
- 1 teaspoon Worcestershire sauce

Cooking Instructions:

1. **Preheat the Oven:**
   - Preheat your oven to 350°F (175°C). Grease a loaf pan or line it with parchment paper for easy removal.
2. **Prepare the Vegetables:**
   - In a medium skillet, sauté the finely chopped onion, green bell pepper, and celery over medium heat until they are tender, about 5-7 minutes. Add the minced garlic and cook for an additional 1-2 minutes until fragrant. Remove from heat and let cool slightly.
3. **Mix the Meatloaf:**
   - In a large mixing bowl, combine the ground beef, ground pork, sautéed vegetables, breadcrumbs, milk, beaten eggs, Worcestershire sauce, Cajun seasoning, dried thyme, dried oregano, paprika, cayenne pepper, black pepper, and salt. Mix well until all ingredients are evenly incorporated, but do not overmix as this can make the meatloaf tough.
4. **Shape the Meatloaf:**
   - Transfer the meat mixture into the prepared loaf pan, pressing down to ensure it is evenly packed.
5. **Prepare the Glaze:**
   - In a small bowl, mix together the ketchup, brown sugar, Dijon mustard, and Worcestershire sauce. Spread half of the glaze mixture over the top of the meatloaf.

6. **Bake the Meatloaf:**
    - Place the loaf pan in the preheated oven and bake for 1 hour, or until the internal temperature reaches 160°F (71°C).
    - About 15 minutes before the meatloaf is done, spread the remaining glaze over the top and continue baking.
7. **Rest and Serve:**
    - Remove the meatloaf from the oven and let it rest for 10-15 minutes before slicing.
    - Serve hot, with your favorite sides such as mashed potatoes, green beans, or a fresh salad.

Chapter 17: Chicken and Sausage Sauce Piquante

A tangy, spicy tomato-based stew with chicken and sausage, served over rice.

Ingredients

- 1 whole chicken, cut into serving pieces
- 1 pound smoked sausage, sliced
- 1/2 cup vegetable oil
- 1/2 cup all-purpose flour
- 2 large onions, chopped
- 1 green bell pepper, chopped
- 1 red bell pepper, chopped
- 3 celery stalks, chopped
- 4 cloves garlic, minced
- 1 can (14.5 oz) diced tomatoes
- 1 can (6 oz) tomato paste
- 1 quart chicken stock
- 2 teaspoons Cajun seasoning
- 1 teaspoon paprika
- 1/2 teaspoon cayenne pepper (optional for extra heat)
- 2 bay leaves
- 1/2 cup green onions, chopped
- 1/4 cup fresh parsley, chopped
- Salt and pepper to taste
- Cooked white rice, for serving

Instructions

1. **Prepare the Roux:**
    - In a large, heavy-bottomed pot or Dutch oven, heat the vegetable oil

over medium heat. Gradually whisk in the flour to form a roux. Continue to cook, stirring constantly, until the roux reaches a dark brown color, about 15-20 minutes. Be patient and careful not to burn the roux.
2. **Sauté Vegetables:**
    - Once the roux is ready, add the chopped onions, green bell pepper, red bell pepper, and celery to the pot. Cook, stirring frequently, until the vegetables are softened, about 5-7 minutes.
3. **Add Garlic and Tomatoes:**
    - Stir in the minced garlic and cook for another minute until fragrant. Then, add the diced tomatoes and tomato paste, stirring well to combine.
4. **Add Chicken and Sausage:**
    - Add the chicken pieces and sliced sausage to the pot. Cook, stirring occasionally, until the chicken is browned on all sides, about 10 minutes.
5. **Simmer:**
    - Pour in the chicken stock, then add the Cajun seasoning, paprika, cayenne pepper (if using), and bay leaves. Bring the mixture to a boil, then reduce the heat to low and let it simmer for about 1.5 to 2 hours, or until the chicken is tender and cooked through. Stir occasionally to prevent sticking.

6. **Add Final Ingredients:**
    - About 10 minutes before serving, stir in the chopped green onions and parsley. Season the sauce piquante with salt and pepper to taste.
7. **Serve:**
    - Serve the chicken and sausage sauce piquante over cooked white rice. Enjoy this flavorful and spicy Cajun dish!

Chapter 18: Andouille Sausage

A smoked sausage made from pork and seasoned with garlic, pepper, onions, and wine.

Ingredients

- 5 pounds pork shoulder, cut into 1-inch cubes
- 1 pound pork fat, cut into 1-inch cubes
- 1/4 cup garlic, minced
- 2 tablespoons kosher salt
- 1 tablespoon black pepper
- 1 tablespoon paprika
- 1 tablespoon onion powder
- 1 tablespoon garlic powder
- 1 teaspoon cayenne pepper
- 1 teaspoon dried thyme
- 1 teaspoon dried oregano
- 1 teaspoon dried sage
- 1/2 teaspoon crushed red pepper flakes
- 1/2 cup cold water
- 10 feet hog casings, soaked in warm water and rinsed

Instructions

1. **Prepare the Meat:**
    - In a large bowl, combine the pork shoulder and pork fat. Pass the meat and fat through a meat grinder fitted with a coarse plate. If you don't have a grinder, you can use pre-ground pork but ensure it has a good fat content.

2. **Season the Meat:**
    - Add the minced garlic, kosher salt, black pepper, paprika, onion powder, garlic powder, cayenne pepper, thyme, oregano, sage, and crushed red pepper flakes to the ground meat. Mix thoroughly to evenly distribute the spices.
3. **Add Water:**
    - Gradually add the cold water to the seasoned meat mixture, mixing well with your hands or a stand mixer fitted with a paddle attachment. The mixture should be sticky and hold together well.
4. **Stuff the Sausage:**
    - Rinse the hog casings thoroughly under cold water. Fit a sausage stuffer with a medium sausage stuffing tube and slide one end of the casing onto the tube. Leave a few inches of casing hanging off the end.
    - Stuff the sausage mixture into the casings, being careful not to overfill. Twist the sausages into 6-inch links as you go, or leave them as one long coil.
5. **Dry the Sausages:**
    - Once all the sausages are stuffed, prick them all over with a pin to remove any air bubbles. Hang the sausages in a cool, well-ventilated area to dry for about 1 hour.

6. **Smoke the Sausages:**
    - Preheat a smoker to 200°F (93°C). Add your choice of wood chips (hickory, oak, or pecan work well for andouille). Place the sausages in the smoker and smoke until they reach an internal temperature of 160°F (71°C), which should take about 2-3 hours.
7. **Cool and Store:**
    - Once the sausages are smoked, let them cool to room temperature. Store in the refrigerator for up to a week or freeze for longer storage.
8. **Serve:**
    - Andouille sausage can be enjoyed in a variety of dishes, such as gumbo, jambalaya, or simply grilled and served with mustard and crusty bread.

Chapter 19: Beignets

Deep-fried dough squares dusted with powdered sugar, a popular sweet treat.

Ingredients:

- 2 1/4 tsp active dry yeast (1 packet)
- 1 1/2 cups warm water (110°F/45°C)
- 1/2 cup granulated sugar
- 1 tsp salt
- 2 large eggs
- 1 cup evaporated milk
- 7 cups all-purpose flour
- 1/4 cup unsalted butter, melted
- Vegetable oil for frying
- Powdered sugar for dusting

Instructions:

1. **Activate the Yeast:**
    - In a large mixing bowl, dissolve the yeast in the warm water. Let it sit for about 5 minutes until it becomes frothy.
2. **Mix the Dough:**
    - Add the sugar, salt, eggs, and evaporated milk to the yeast mixture. Stir to combine.
    - Gradually add 4 cups of the flour, mixing until smooth. Add the melted butter and mix well.
    - Add the remaining 3 cups of flour, one cup at a time, mixing until the

dough comes together and is no longer sticky.
3. **Knead the Dough:**
   o Transfer the dough to a floured surface and knead for about 5-7 minutes, until smooth and elastic.
4. **Let the Dough Rise:**
   o Place the dough in a greased bowl, cover with a damp cloth, and let it rise in a warm, draft-free area for 1 1/2 to 2 hours, or until doubled in size.
5. **Prepare for Frying:**
   o After the dough has risen, punch it down and transfer it to a floured surface. Roll the dough out to a 1/4-inch thickness.
6. **Cut the Beignets:**
   o Using a sharp knife or pizza cutter, cut the dough into 2-inch squares.
7. **Heat the Oil:**
   o In a large, deep pot, heat about 2 inches of vegetable oil to 360°F (182°C).
8. **Fry the Beignets:**
   o Carefully place a few beignet squares into the hot oil, being careful not to overcrowd the pot. Fry until golden brown on each side, about 2-3 minutes per side.
   o Use a slotted spoon to remove the beignets from the oil and drain on paper towels.
9. **Serve:**
   o Generously dust the hot beignets with powdered sugar and serve

immediately. Enjoy with a cup of coffee or hot chocolate!

Chapter 20: Crawfish Pie

A savory pie filled with a mixture of crawfish, vegetables, and spices, baked to perfection.

Ingredients:

- 2 tbsp unsalted butter
- 1 cup finely chopped onions
- 1/2 cup finely chopped bell peppers
- 1/2 cup finely chopped celery
- 2 cloves garlic, minced
- 1 lb crawfish tails, peeled and deveined
- 1/2 cup chicken broth
- 1/2 cup heavy cream
- 2 tbsp all-purpose flour
- 2 tbsp tomato paste
- 1 tsp Cajun seasoning
- 1/2 tsp salt
- 1/2 tsp black pepper
- 1/4 tsp cayenne pepper (optional)
- 2 tbsp chopped parsley
- 2 tbsp chopped green onions
- 1 pre-made pie crust (9-inch, unbaked)
- 1 egg, beaten (for egg wash)

Instructions:

1. **Preheat the Oven:**
    - Preheat your oven to 375°F (190°C).
2. **Prepare the Filling:**
    - In a large skillet, melt the butter over medium heat. Add the chopped onions, bell peppers, and celery. Sauté until the vegetables are soft, about 5-7 minutes.

- Add the minced garlic and cook for another 2 minutes.
3. **Cook the Crawfish:**
    - Add the crawfish tails to the skillet and cook for 2-3 minutes until they turn pink and are cooked through.
4. **Make the Sauce:**
    - In a small bowl, whisk together the chicken broth, heavy cream, and flour until smooth. Add this mixture to the skillet along with the tomato paste, Cajun seasoning, salt, black pepper, and cayenne pepper (if using).
    - Stir well and bring the mixture to a simmer. Cook for 5-7 minutes, until the sauce has thickened.
5. **Add Herbs:**
    - Stir in the chopped parsley and green onions. Remove from heat and let the filling cool slightly.
6. **Assemble the Pie:**
    - Roll out the pre-made pie crust and fit it into a 9-inch pie dish. Trim any excess dough around the edges.
    - Pour the crawfish filling into the pie crust.
7. **Top the Pie:**
    - Roll out the remaining dough to cover the pie. Place it over the filling and crimp the edges to seal. Cut a few small slits in the top crust to allow steam to escape.

8. **Apply Egg Wash:**
    - Brush the top of the pie with the beaten egg to give it a golden brown finish.
9. **Bake:**
    - Place the pie on a baking sheet to catch any drips and bake in the preheated oven for 30-35 minutes, or until the crust is golden brown and the filling is bubbly.
10. **Serve:**
    - Let the pie cool for a few minutes before slicing. Serve warm and enjoy!

Conclusion

Thank you for joining me on this culinary adventure through the vibrant and flavorful world of Cajun cuisine. "20 Classic Cajun Dishes" has brought to your kitchen the essence of Louisiana's rich culinary tradition, offering recipes that are not only delicious but also steeped in history and culture.

As you savor the flavors of these dishes, remember that Cajun cooking is about more than just food; it's about community, celebration, and a love for life. Each recipe in this book has been chosen for its authenticity and ability to bring people together around the table.

I hope these recipes inspire you to explore more of Cajun cuisine and perhaps even create your own variations. May your kitchen be filled with the aromas of spicy and savory dishes, and may your meals be enjoyed with family and friends.

Made in the USA
Columbia, SC
04 November 2024